INTRODUCTION

Our children's coloring book is a delightful way to spark creativity and imagination in young minds. Packed with captivating illustrations and engaging activities, it provides hours of entertainment while encouraging artistic expression.

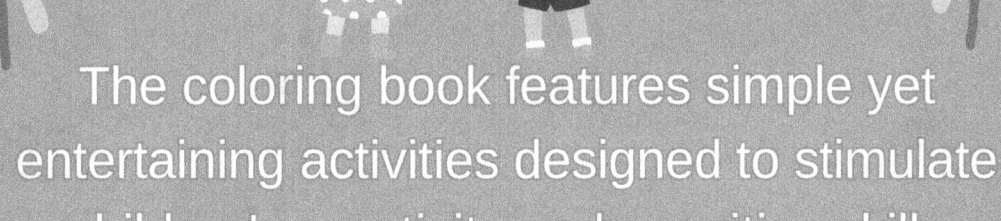

The coloring book features simple yet entertaining activities designed to stimulate children's creativity and cognitive skills

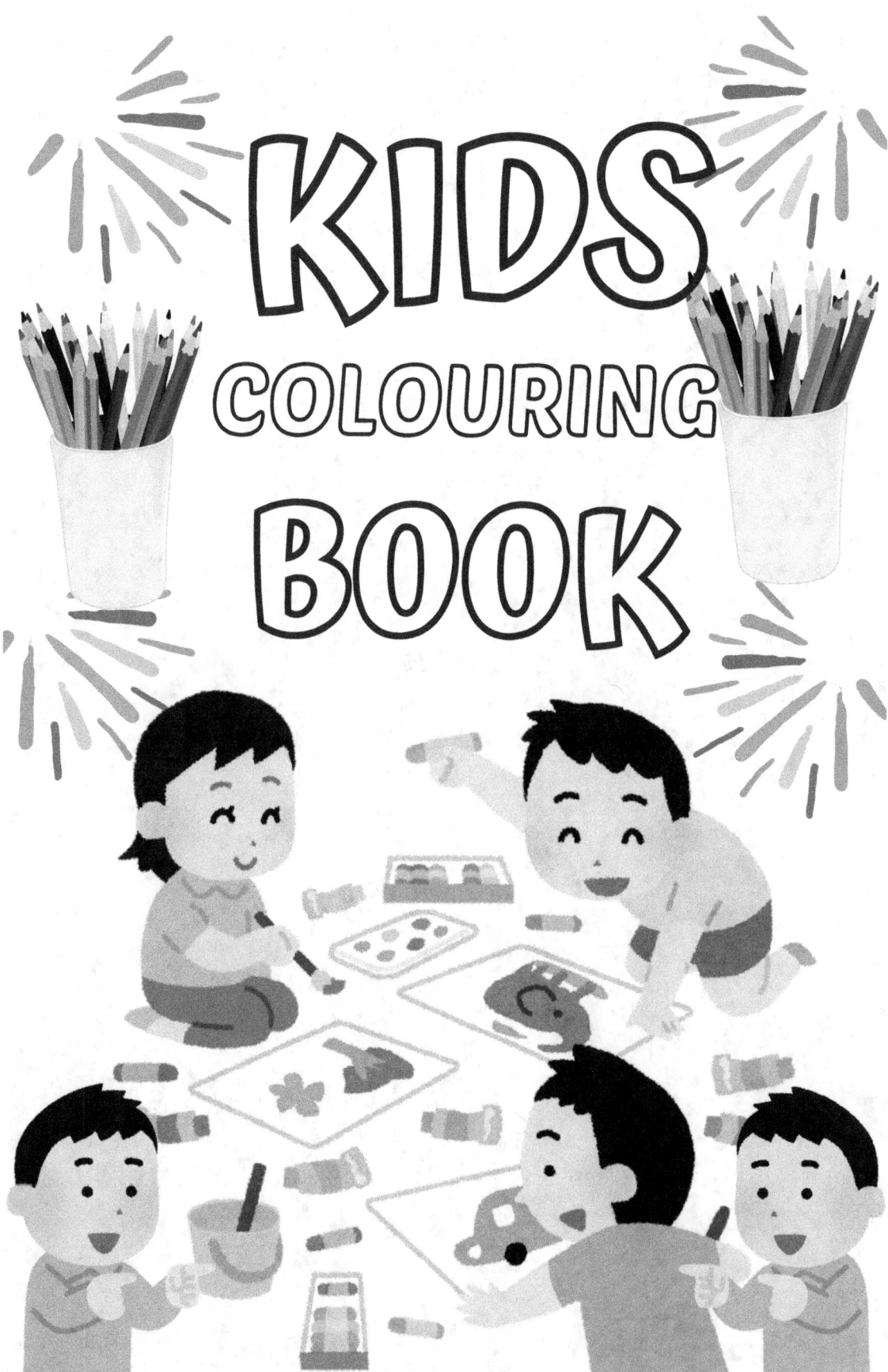

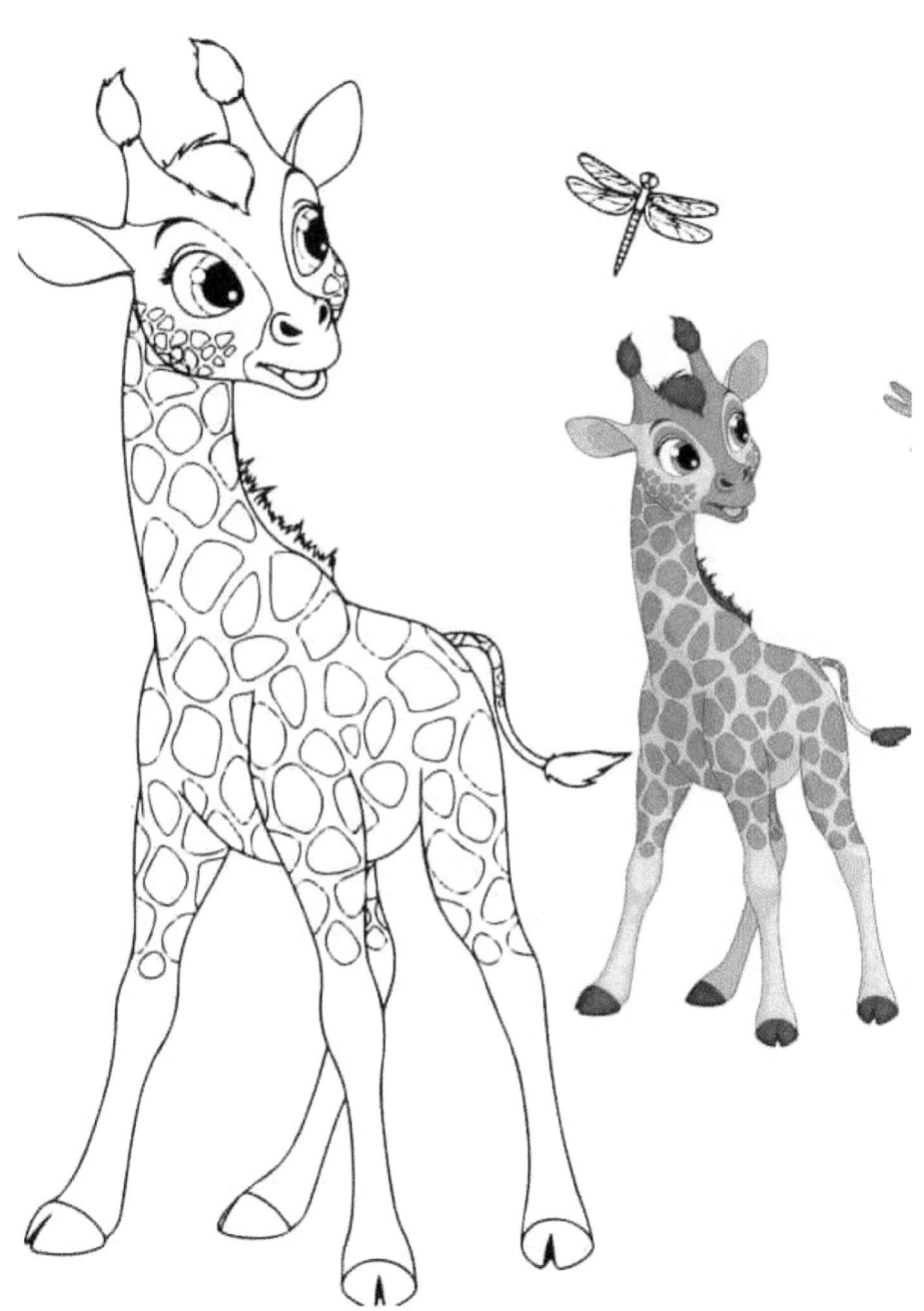

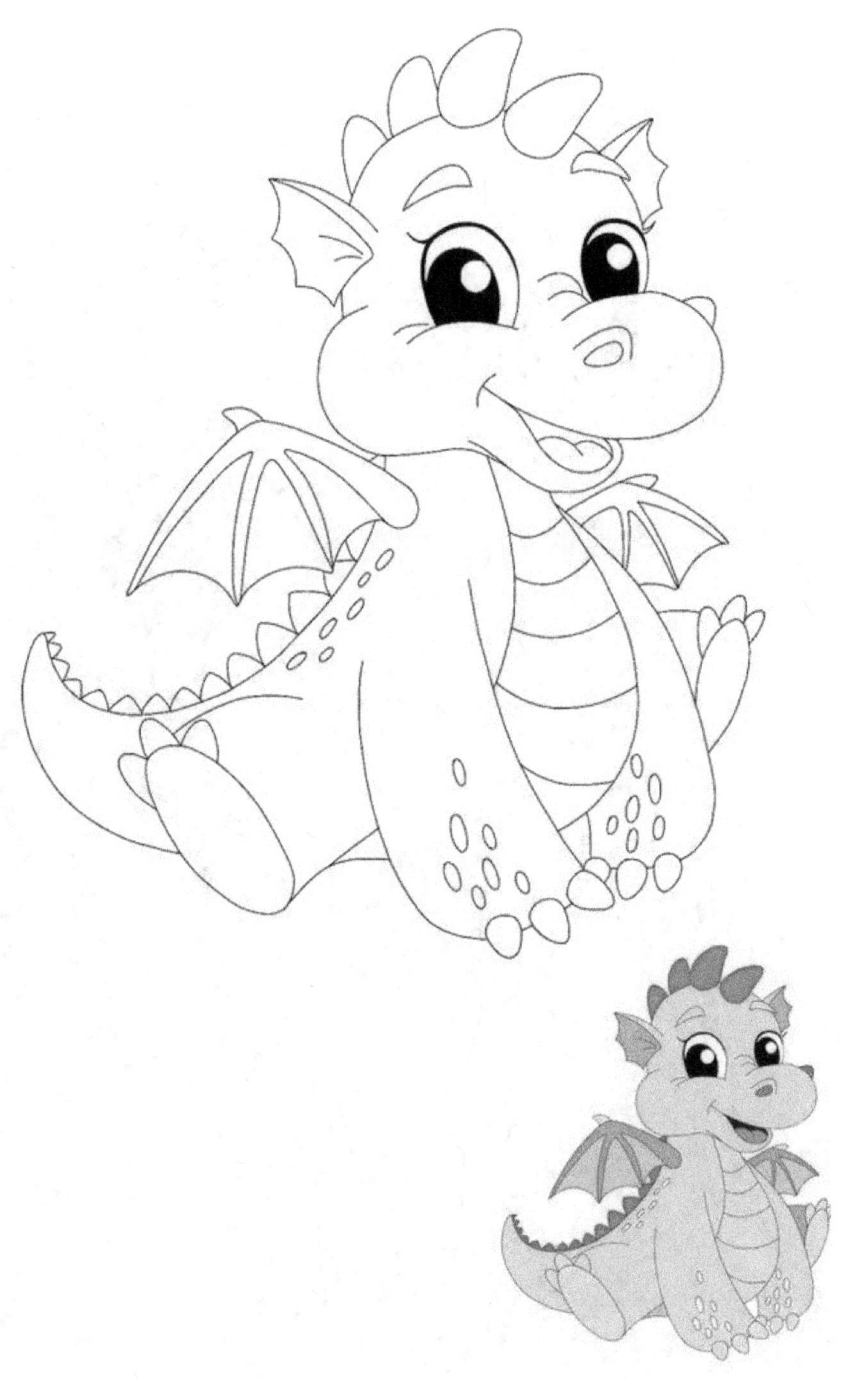

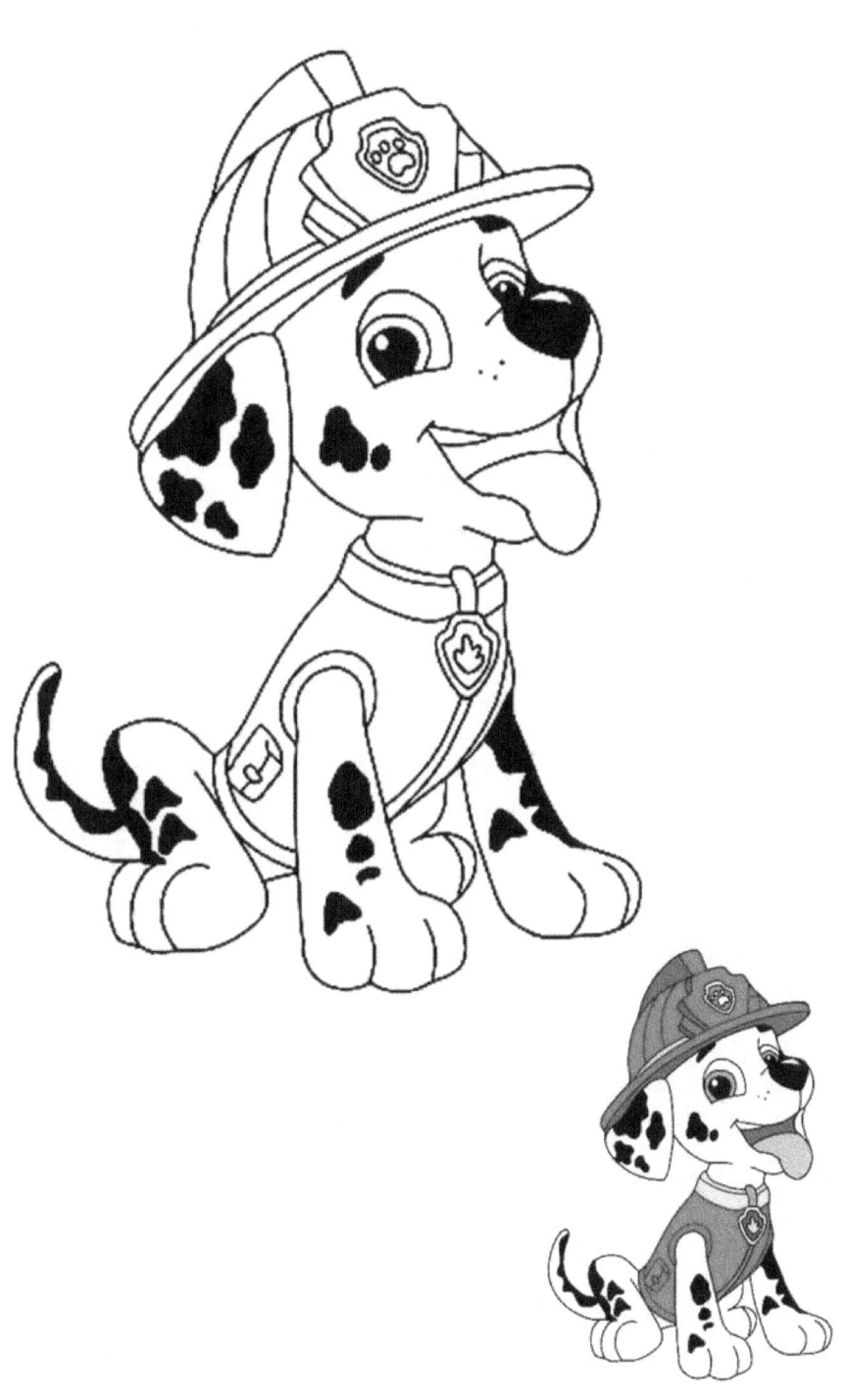

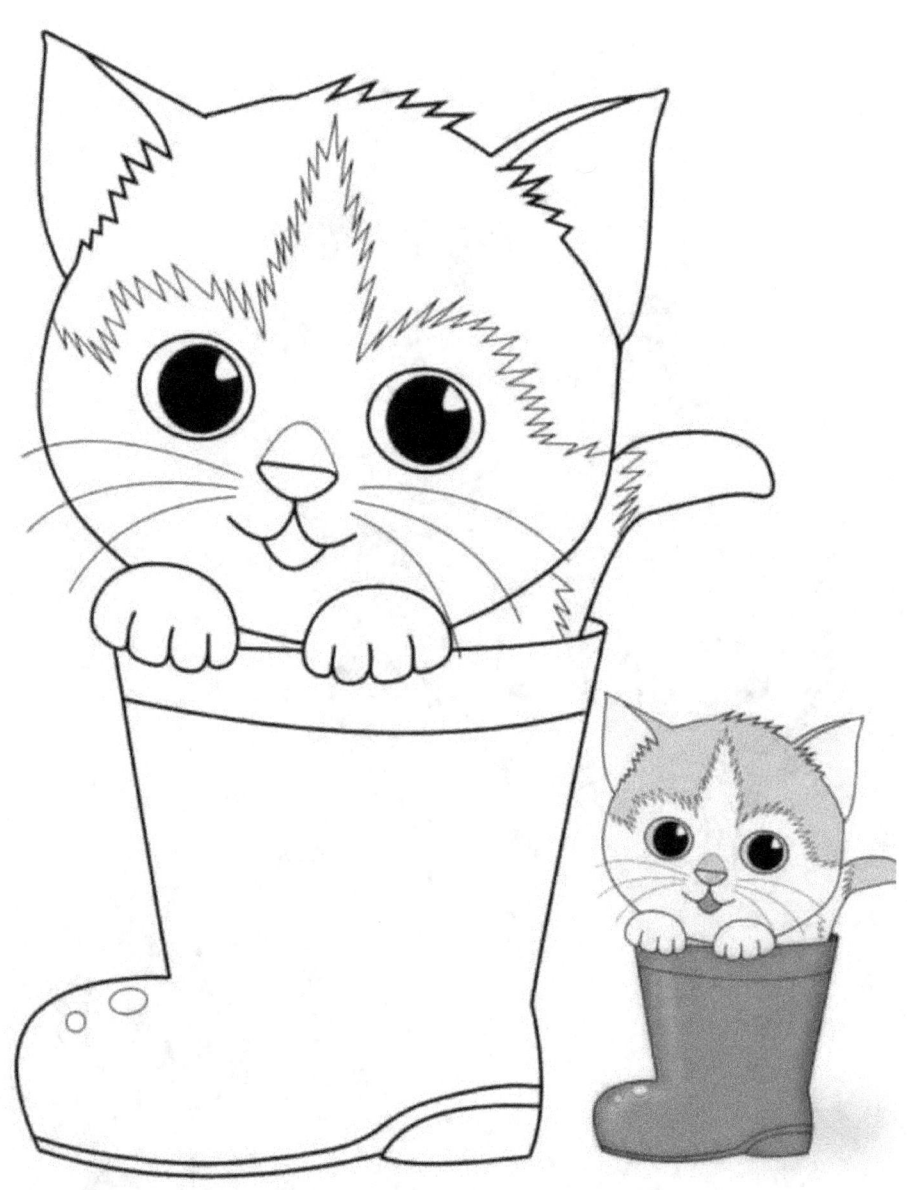

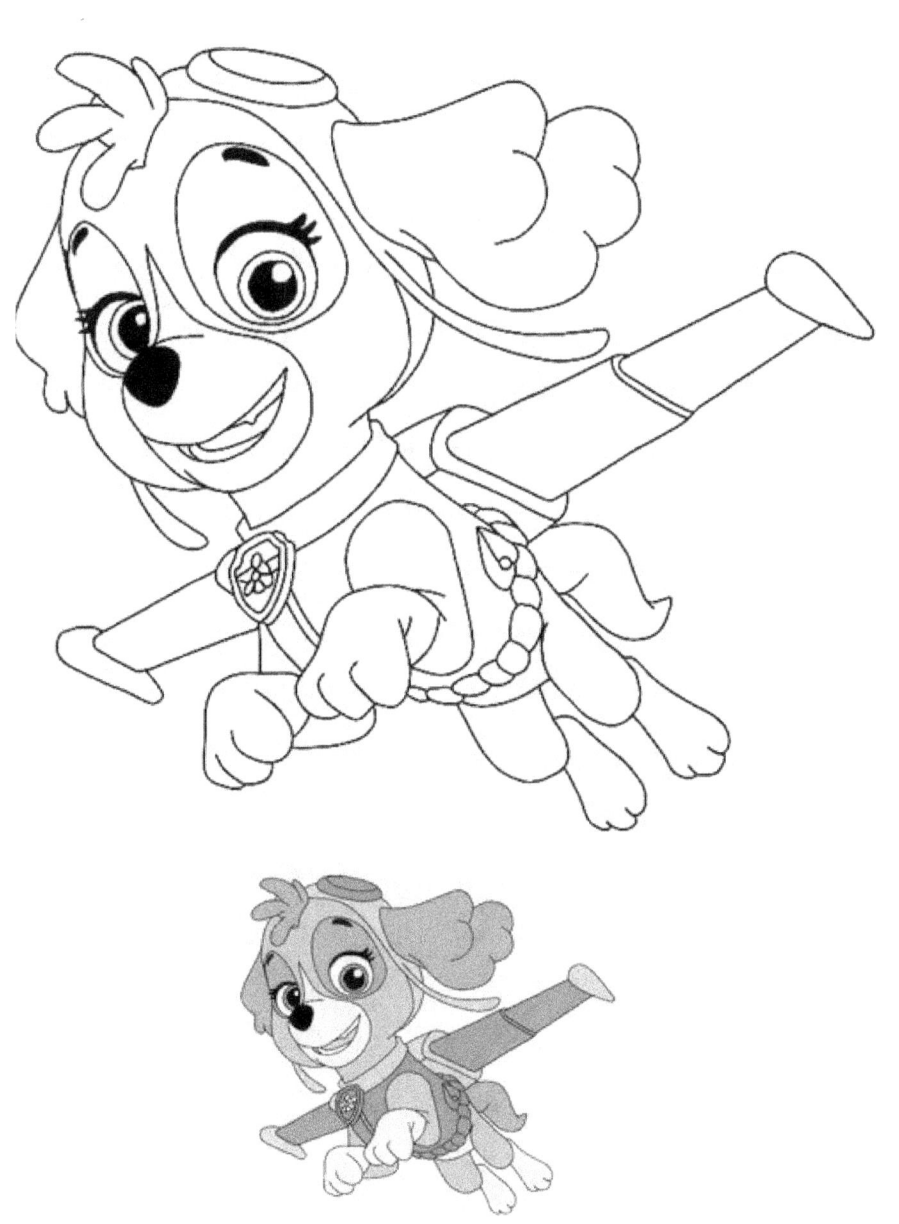

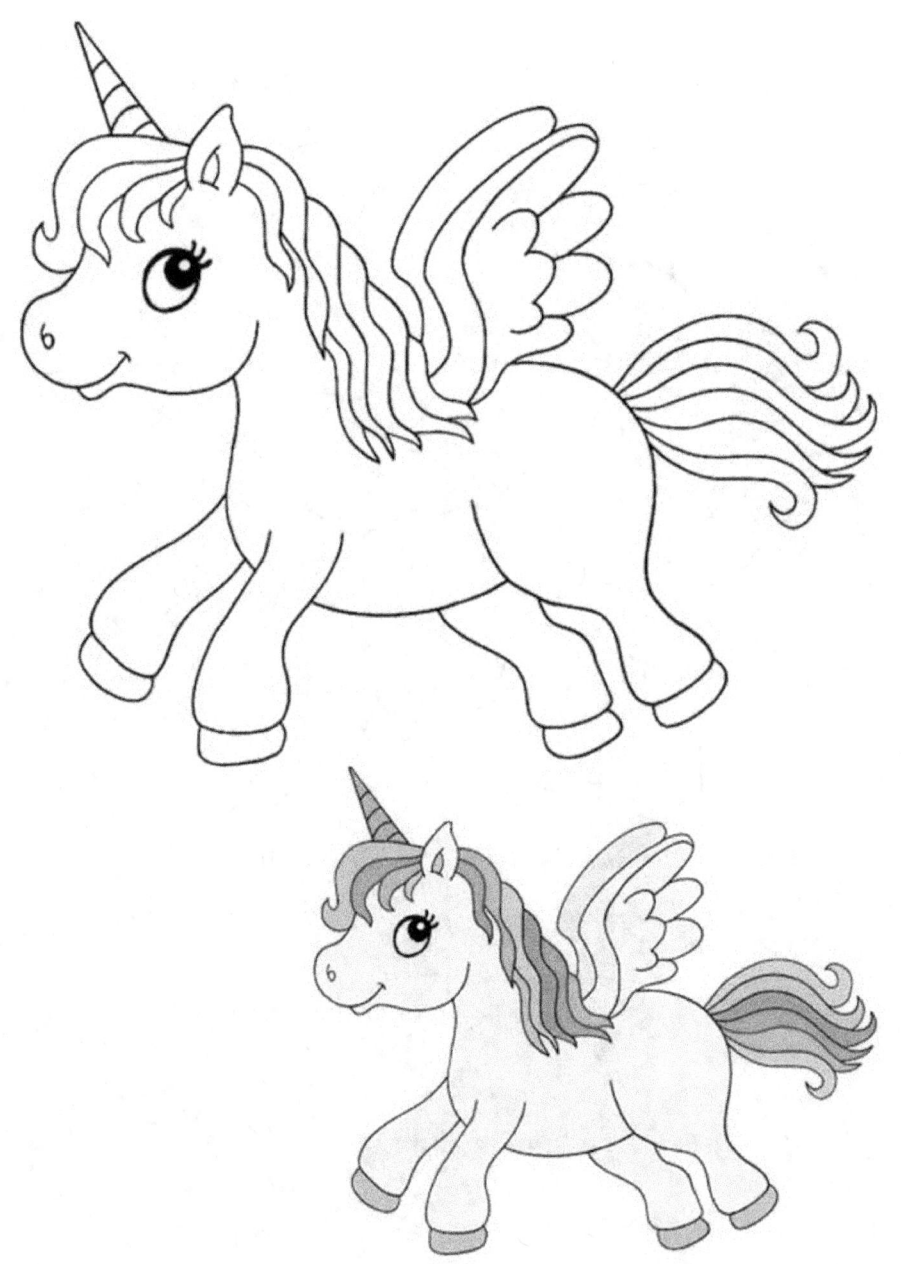

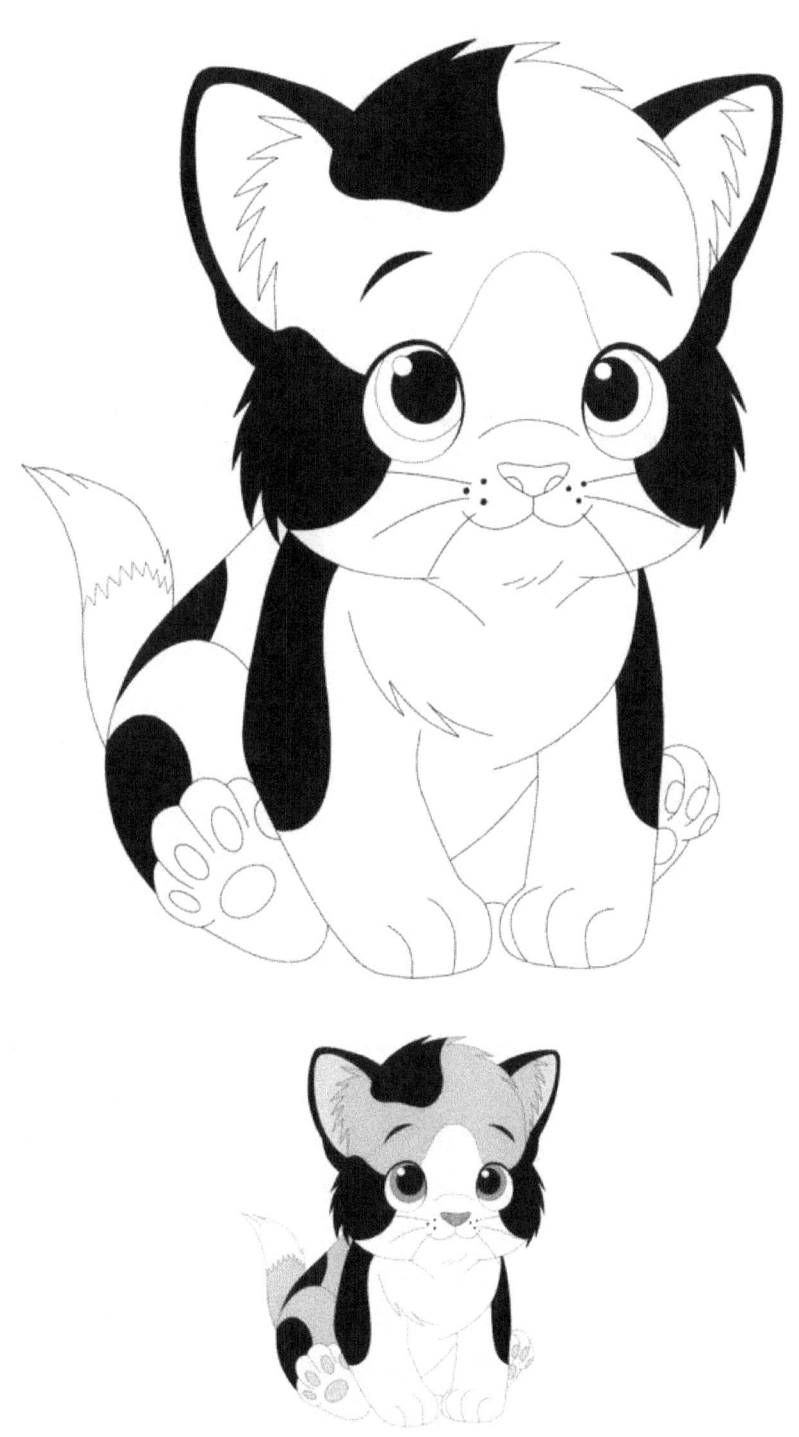

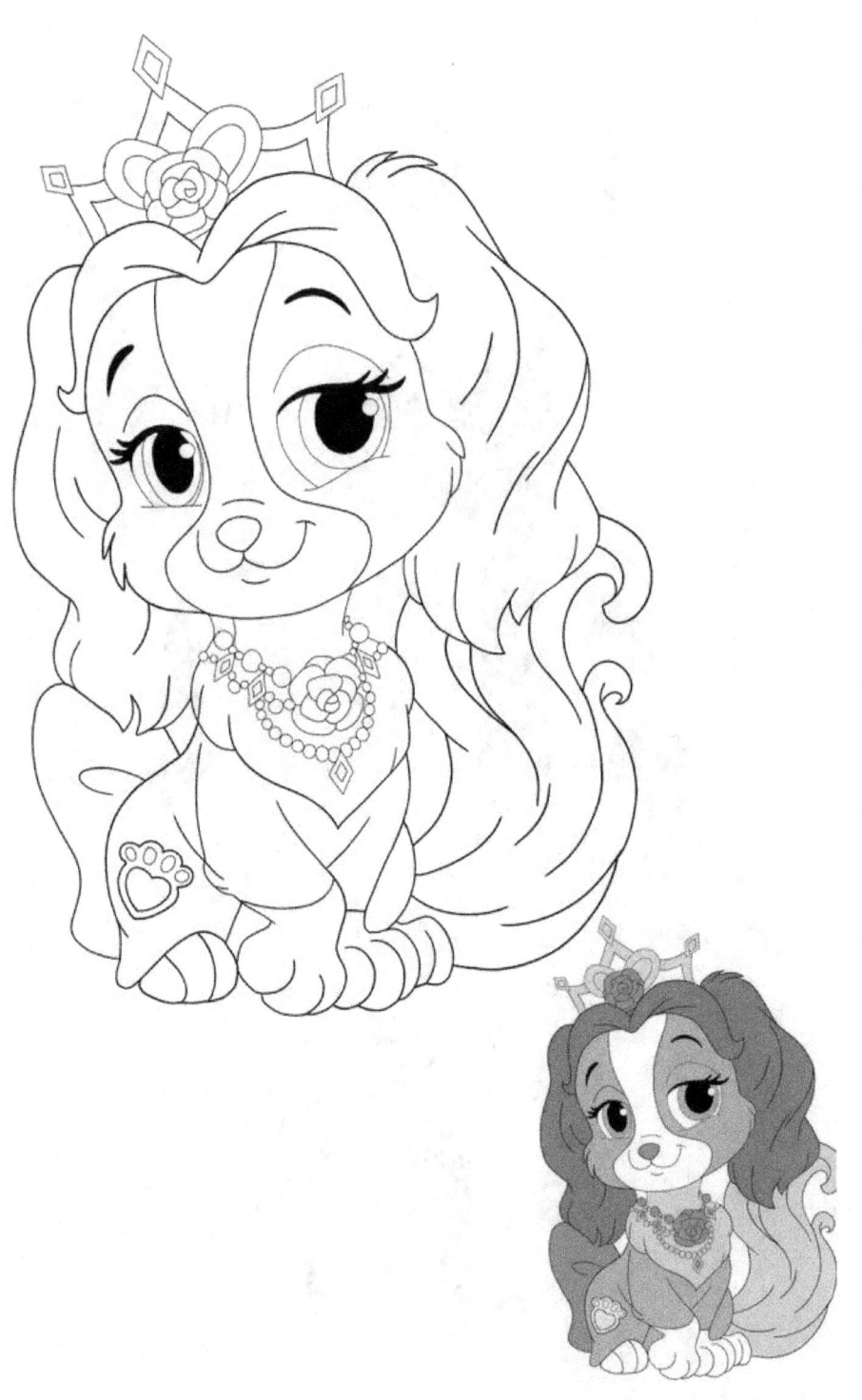

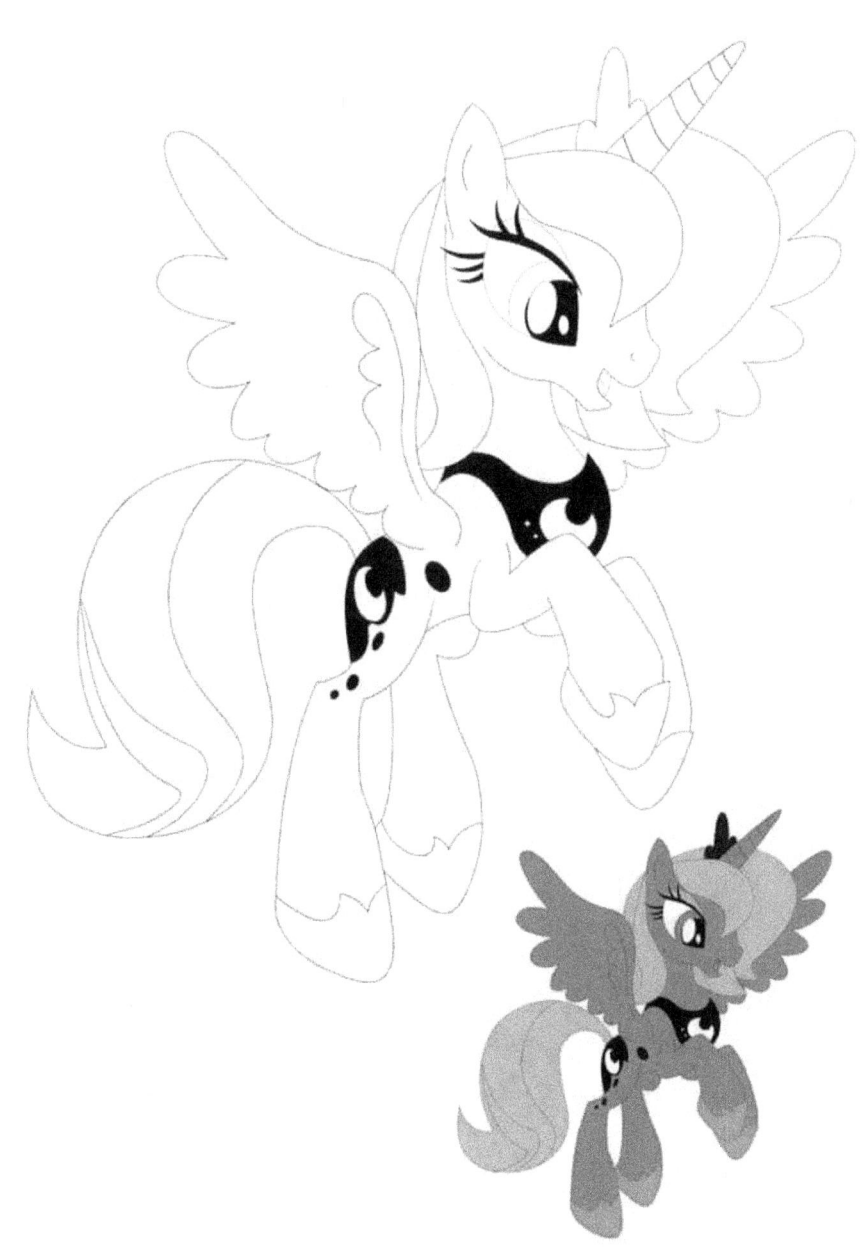

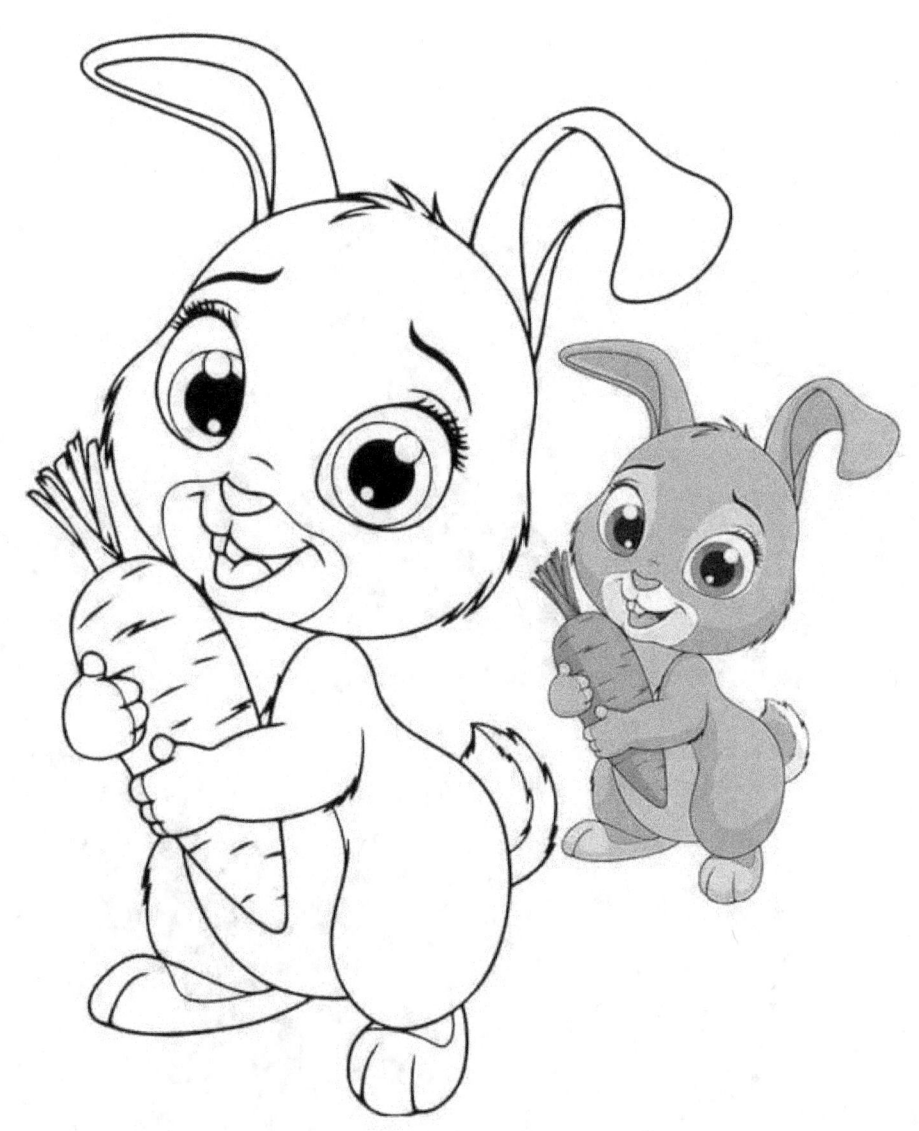

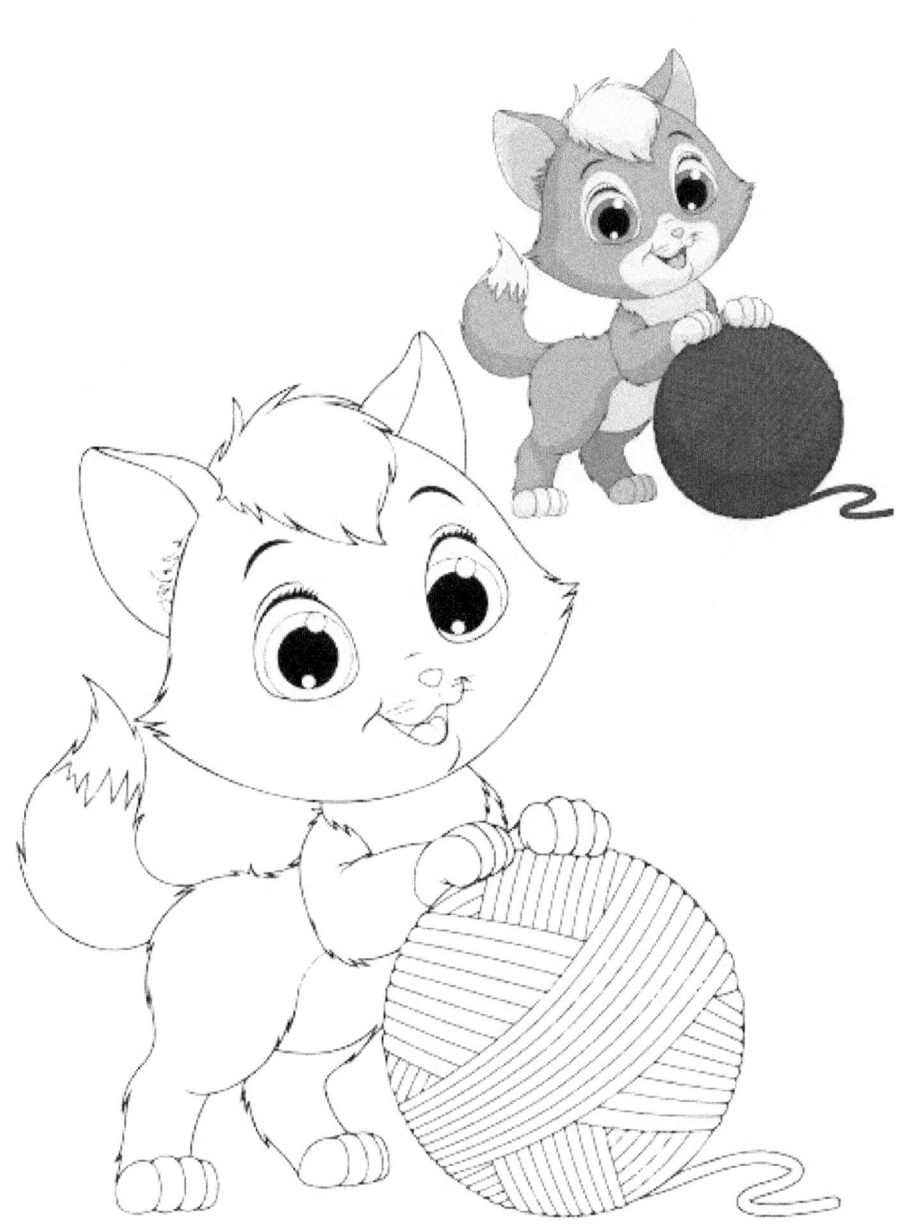

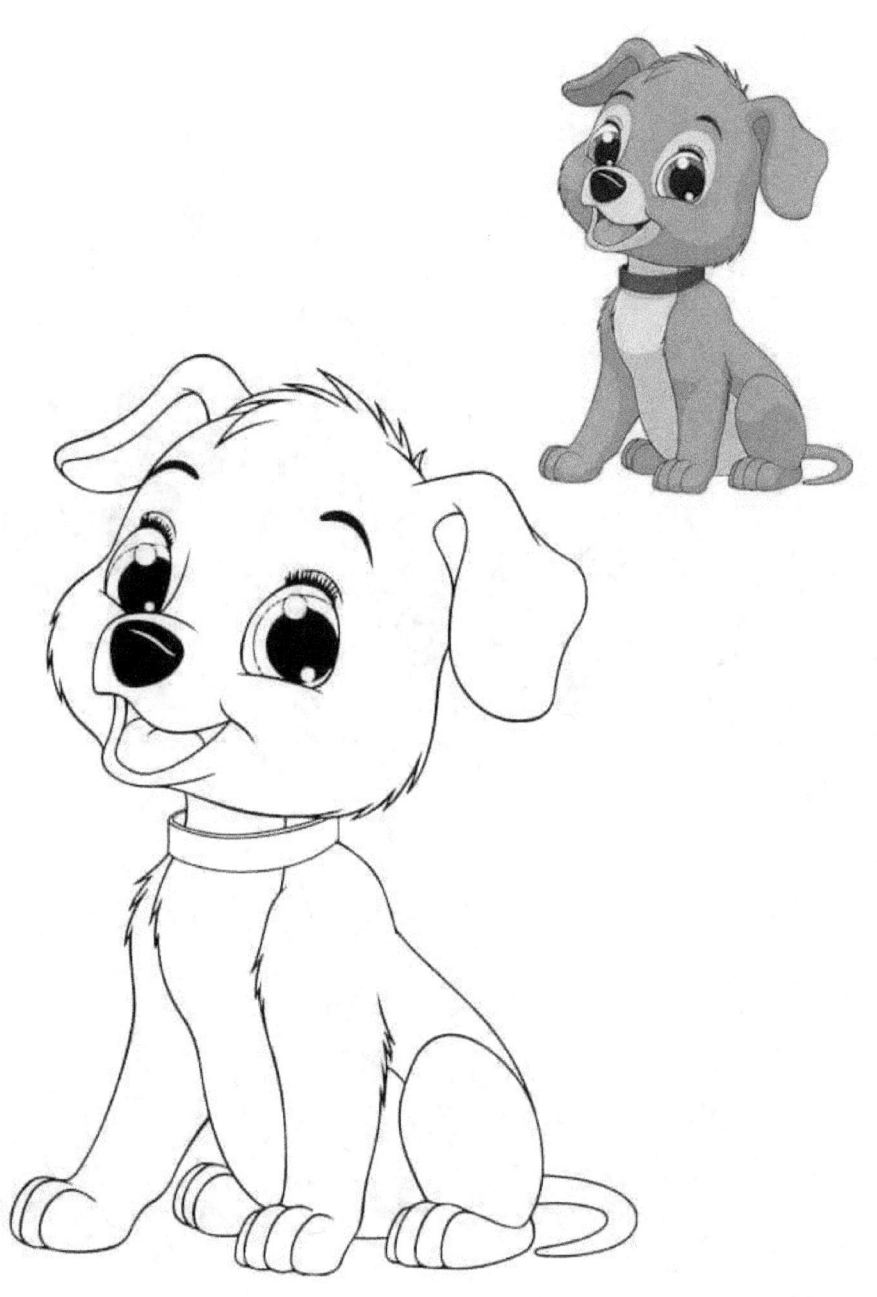

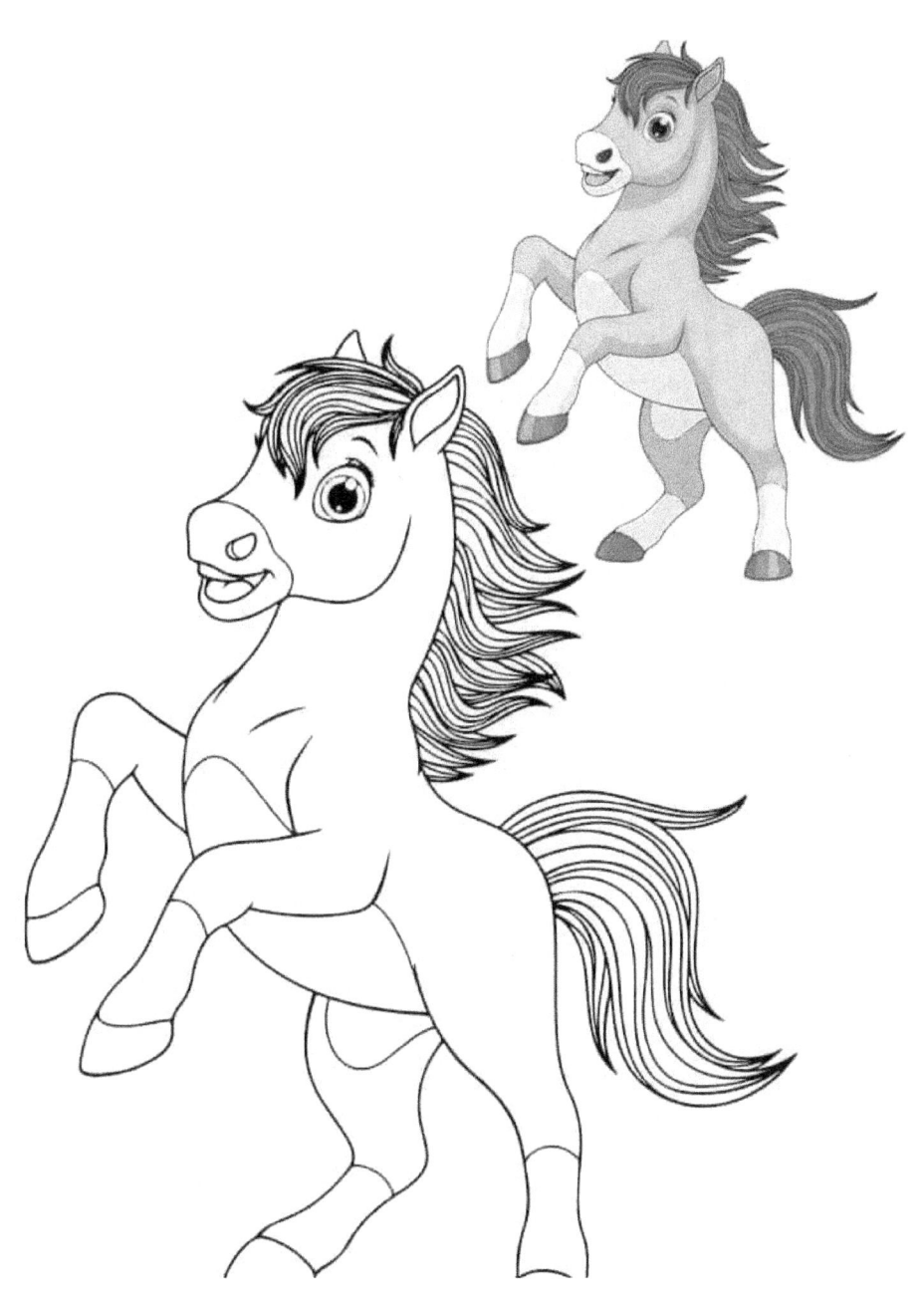

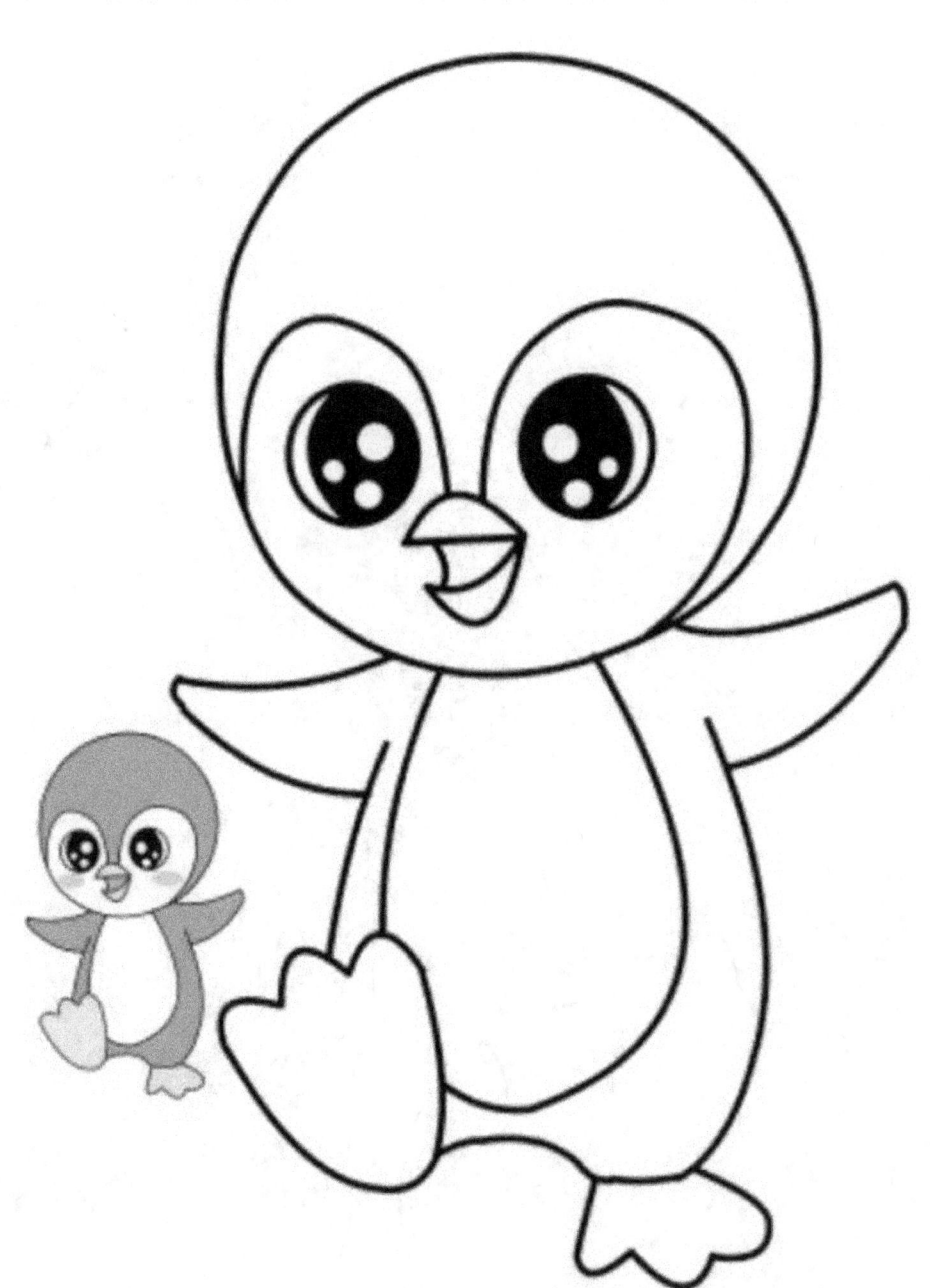

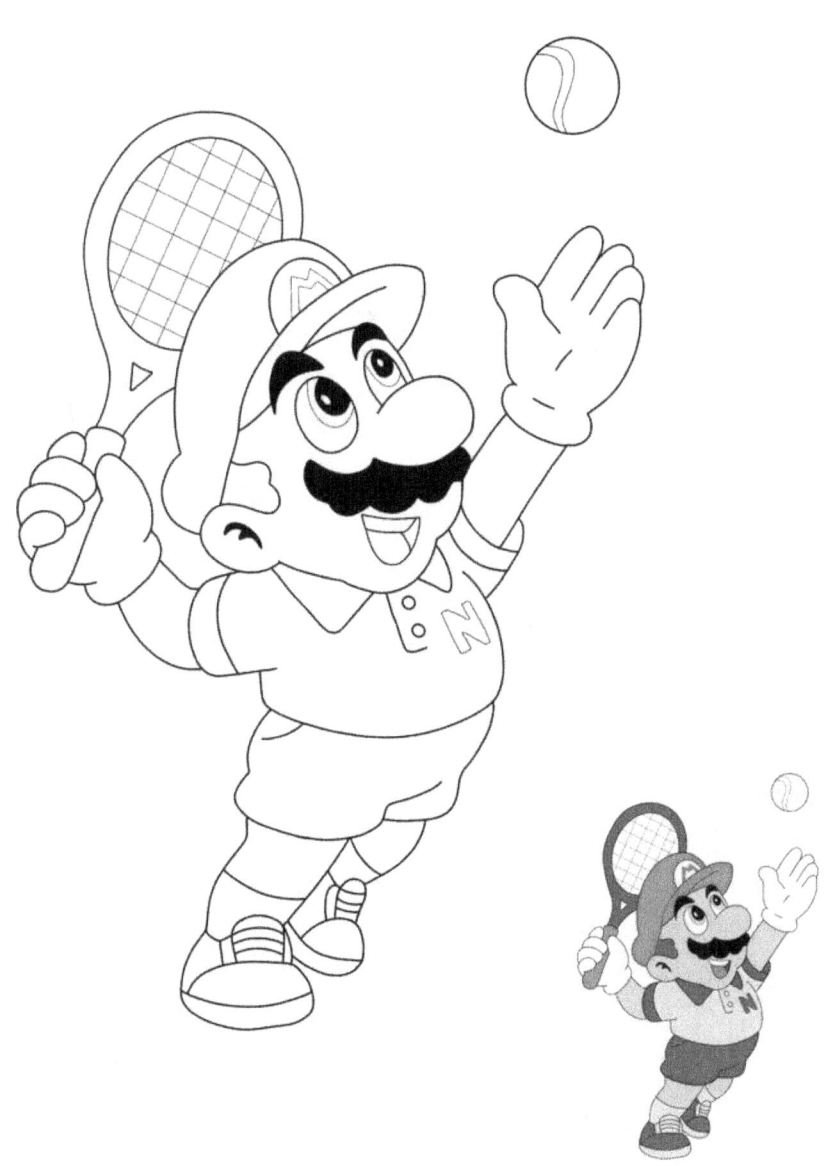

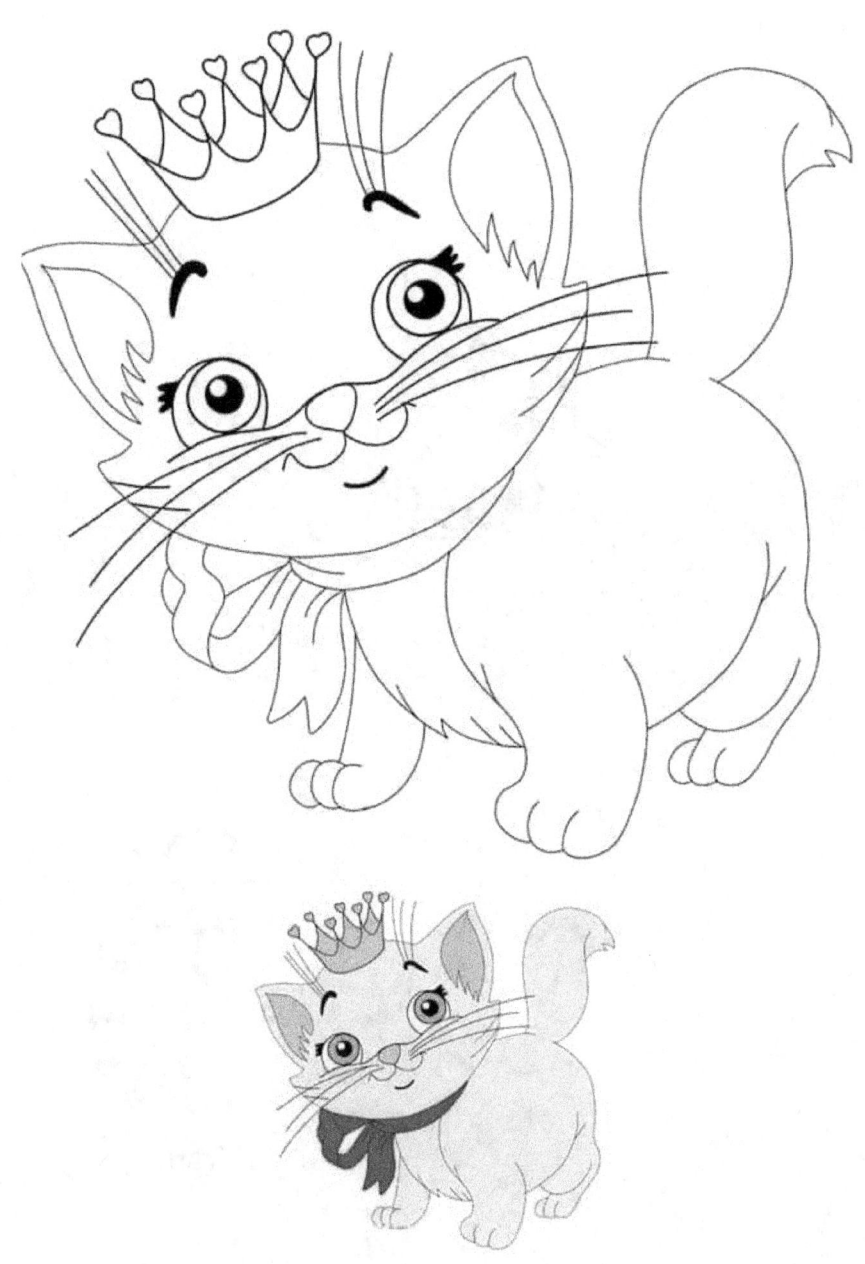

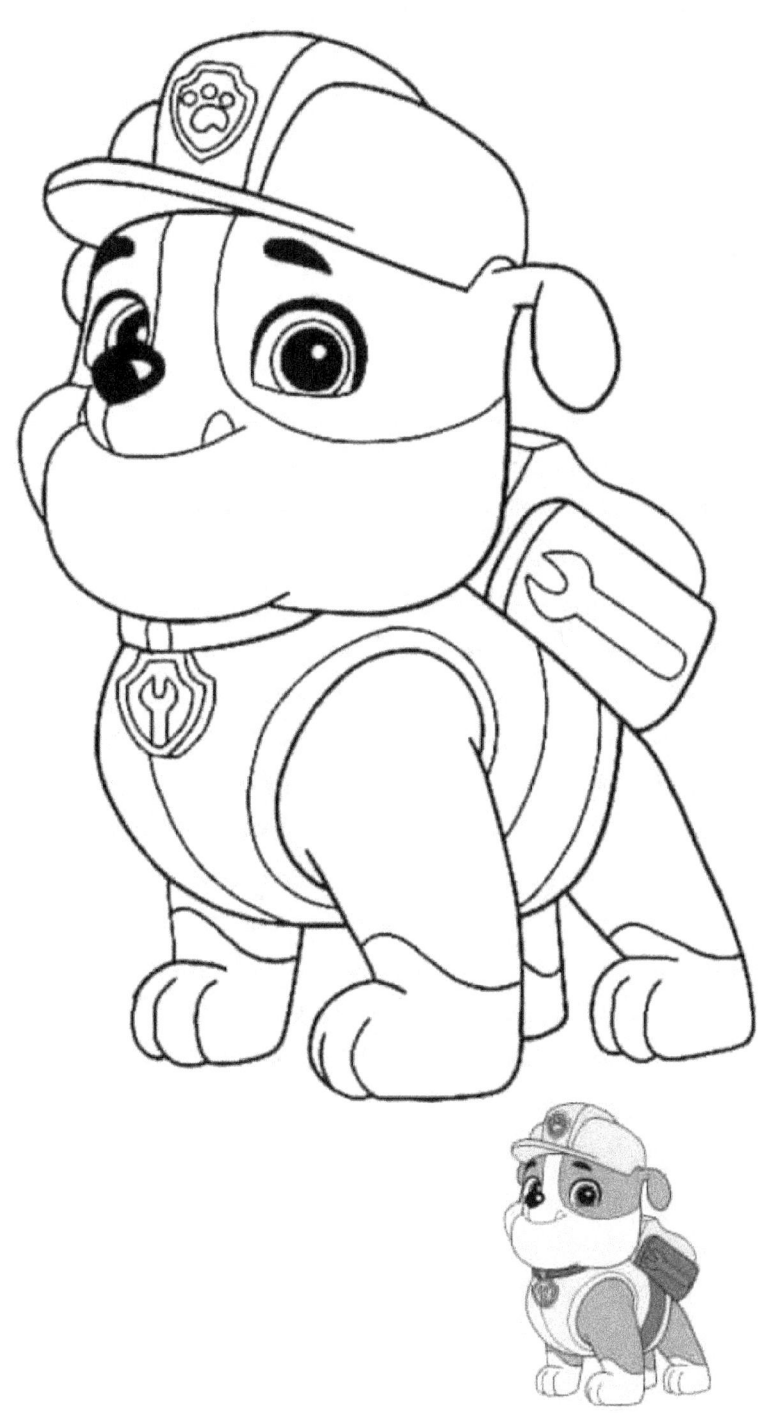

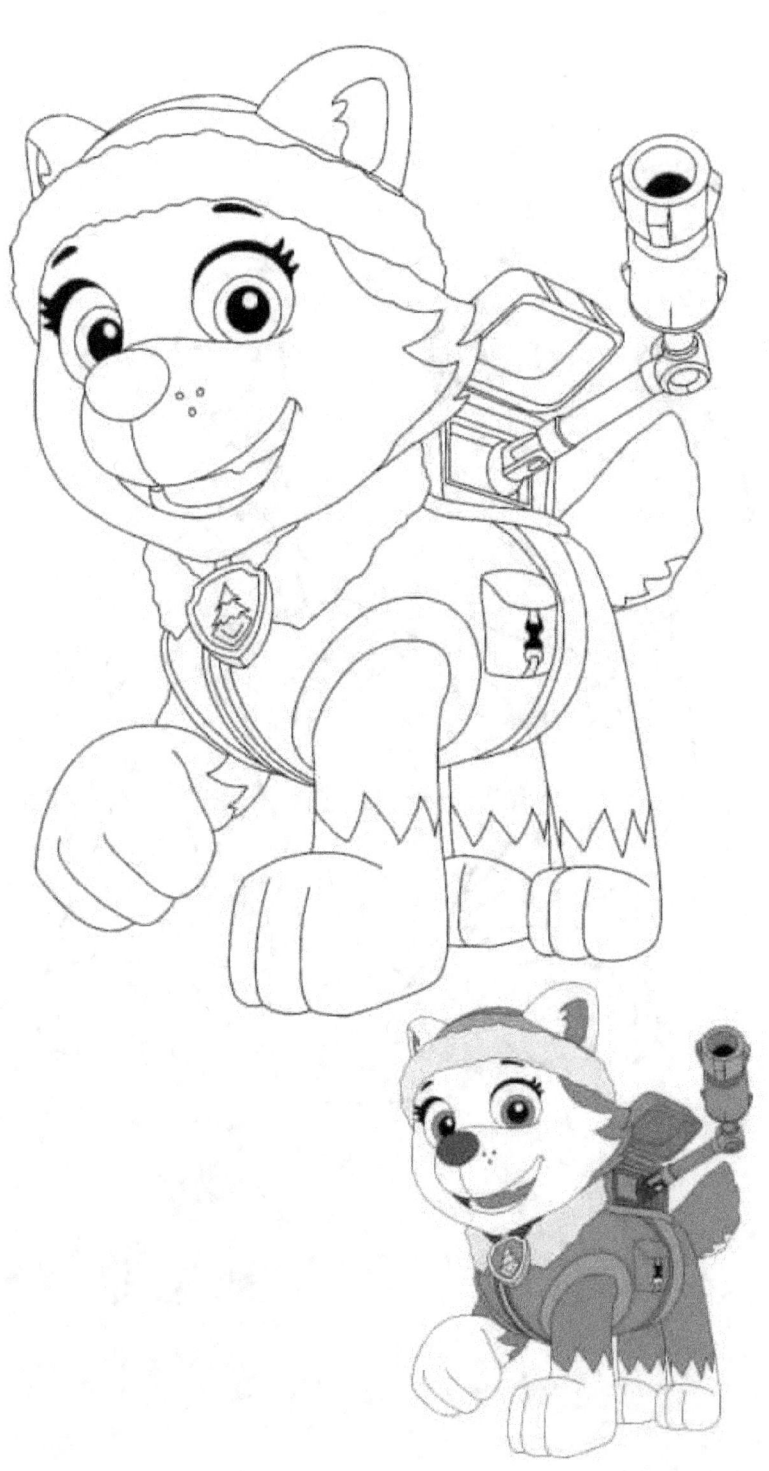

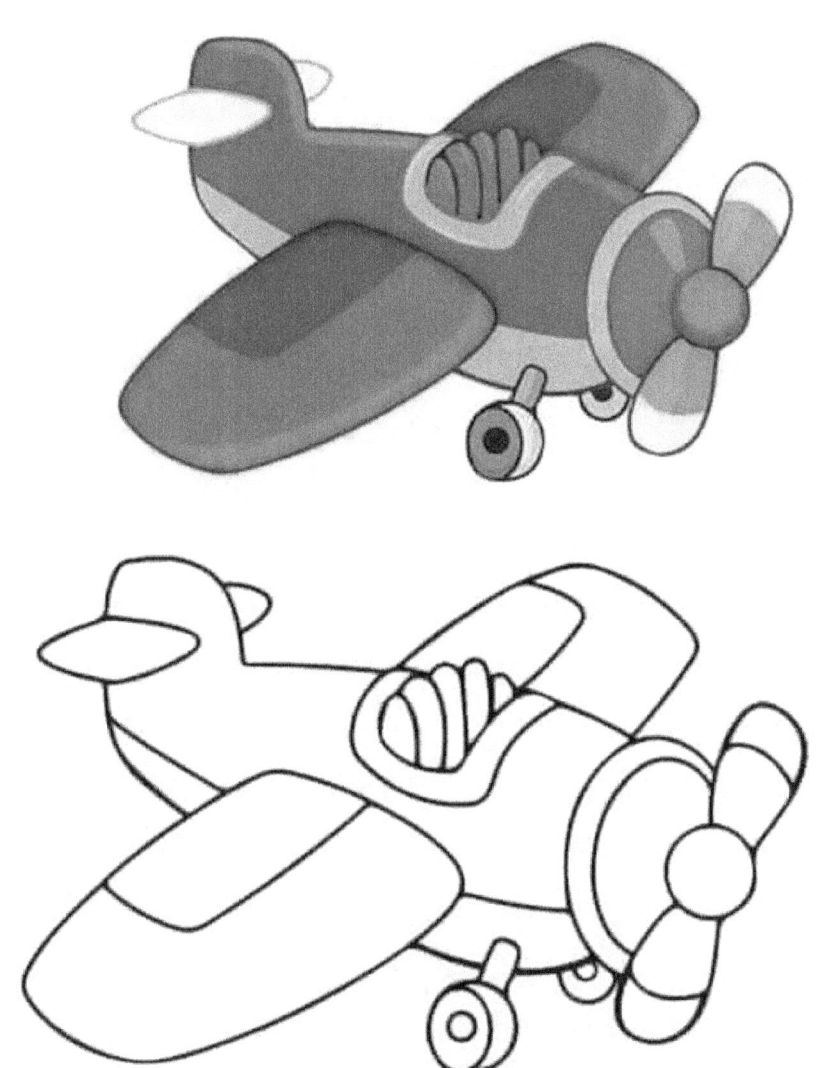

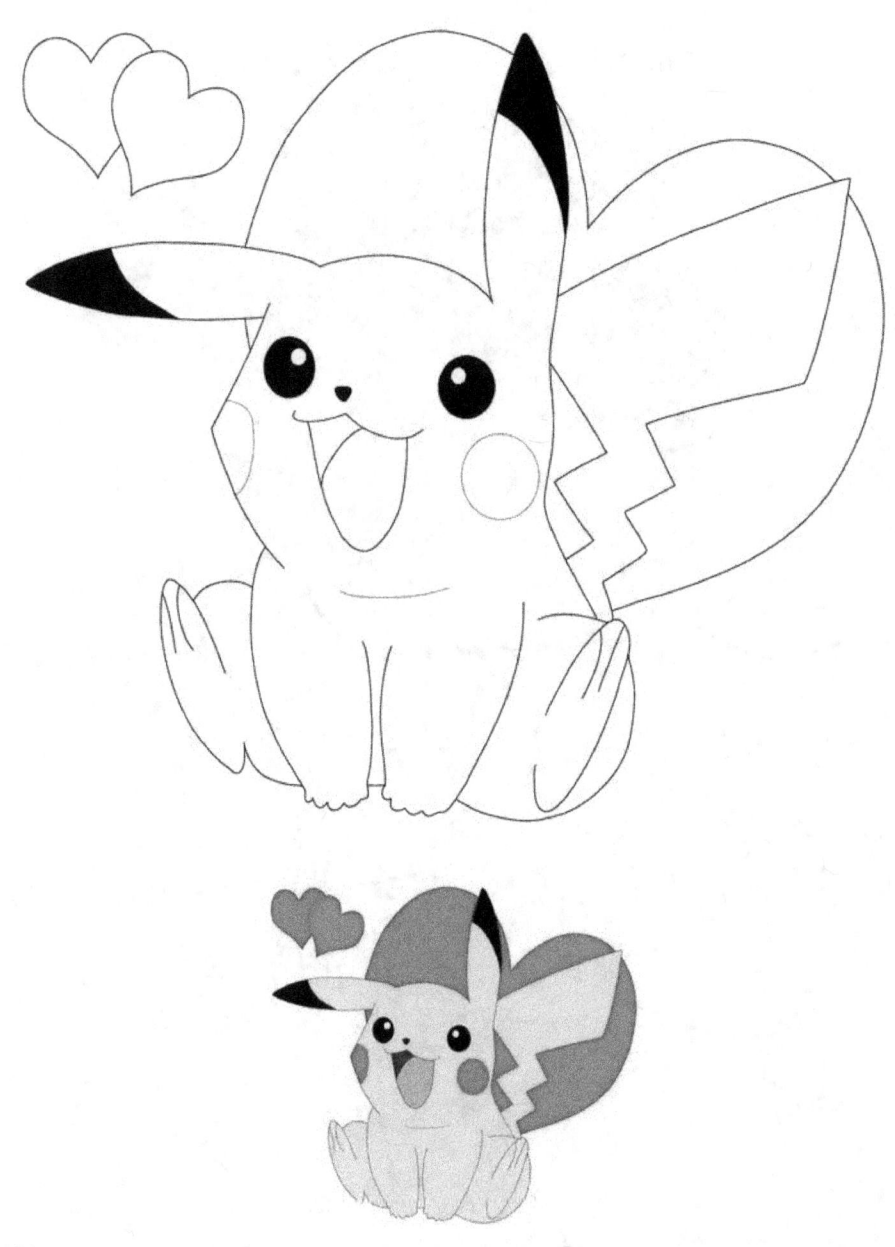

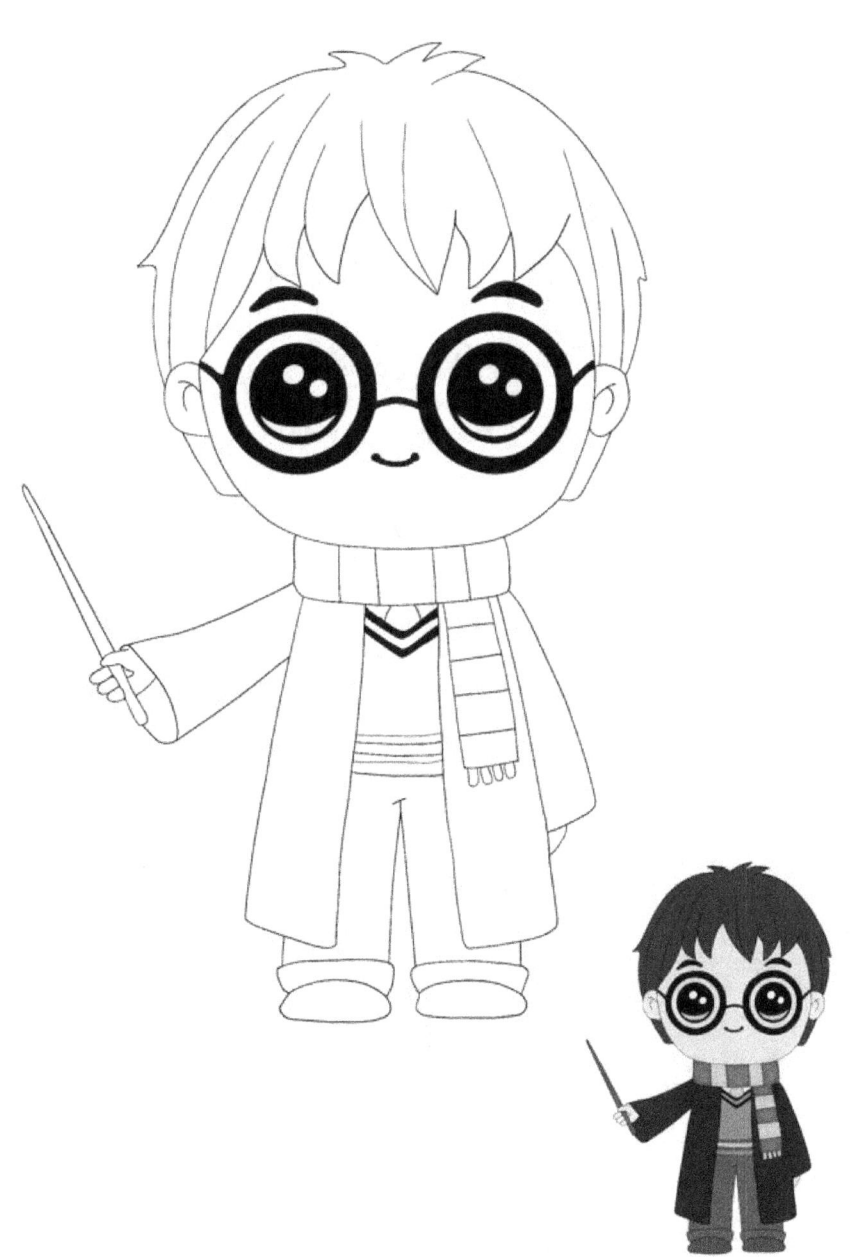

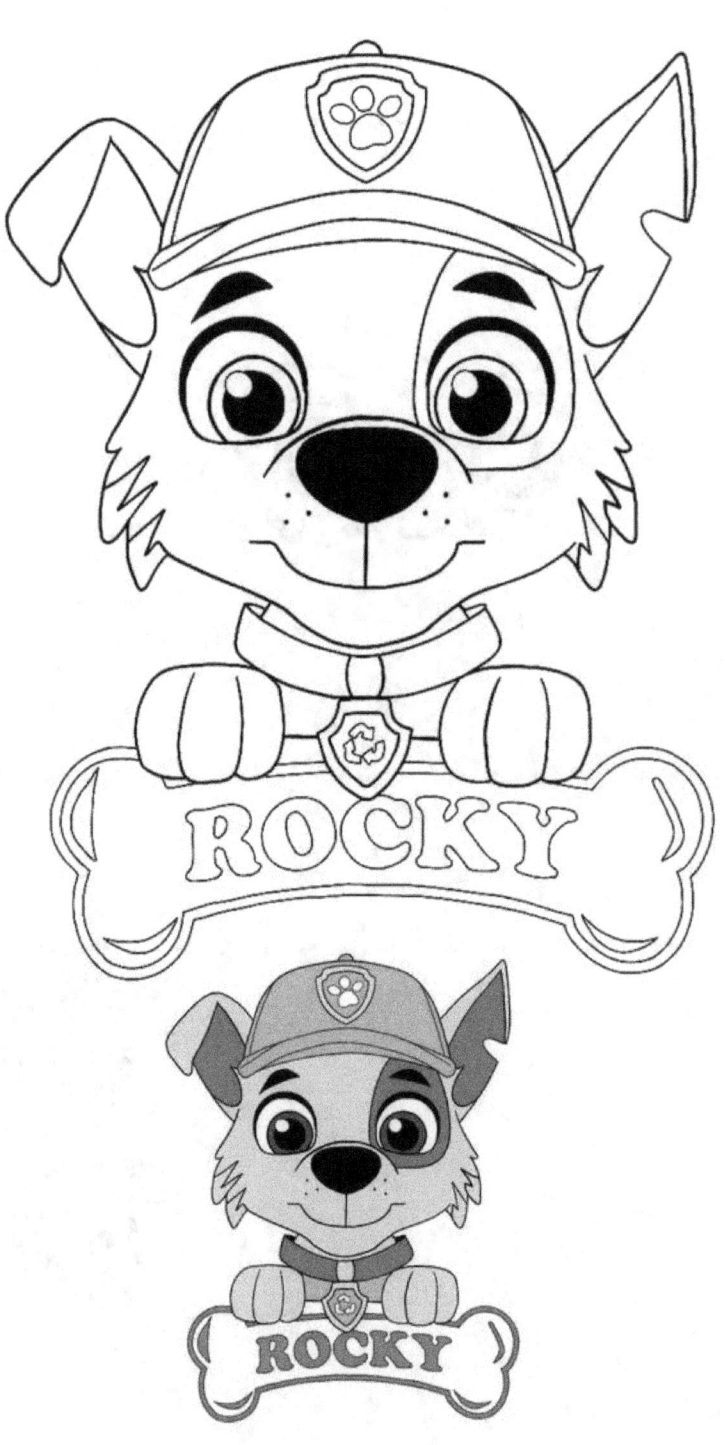

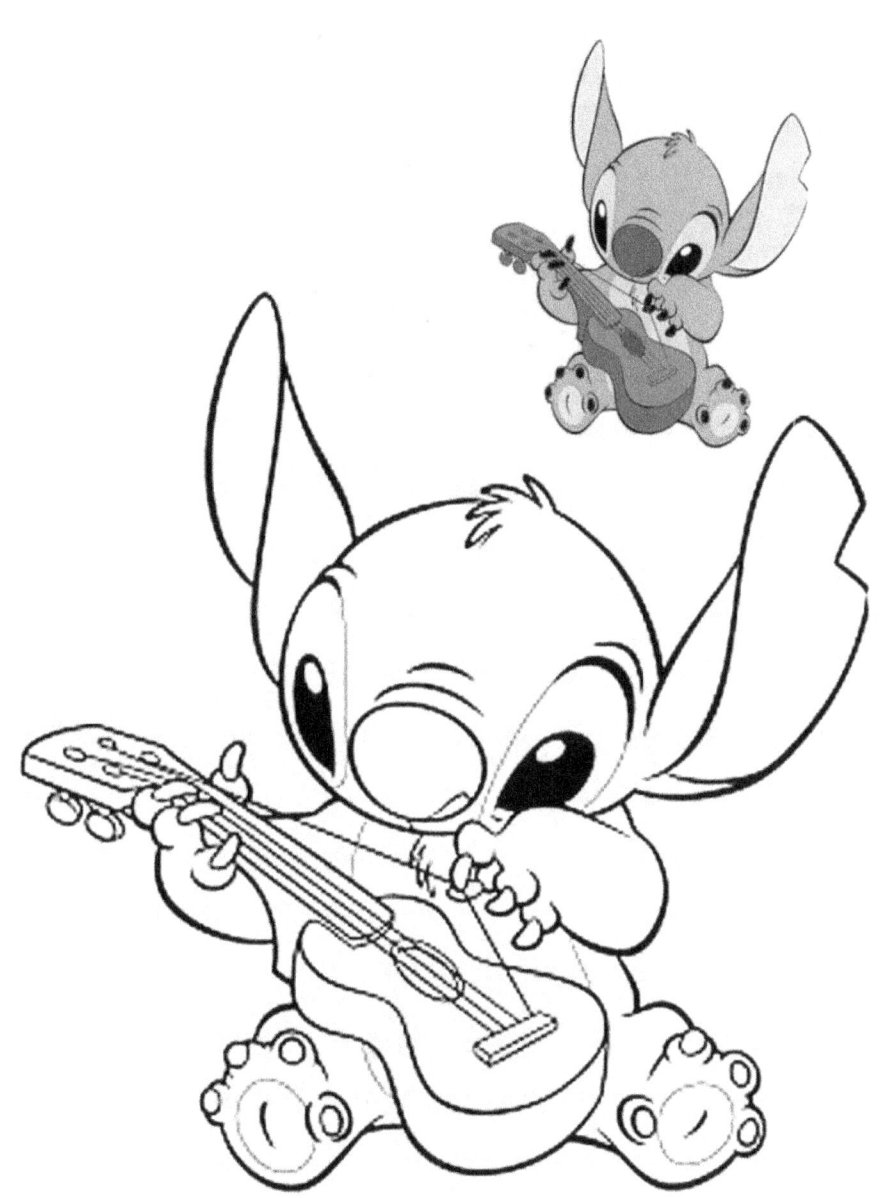

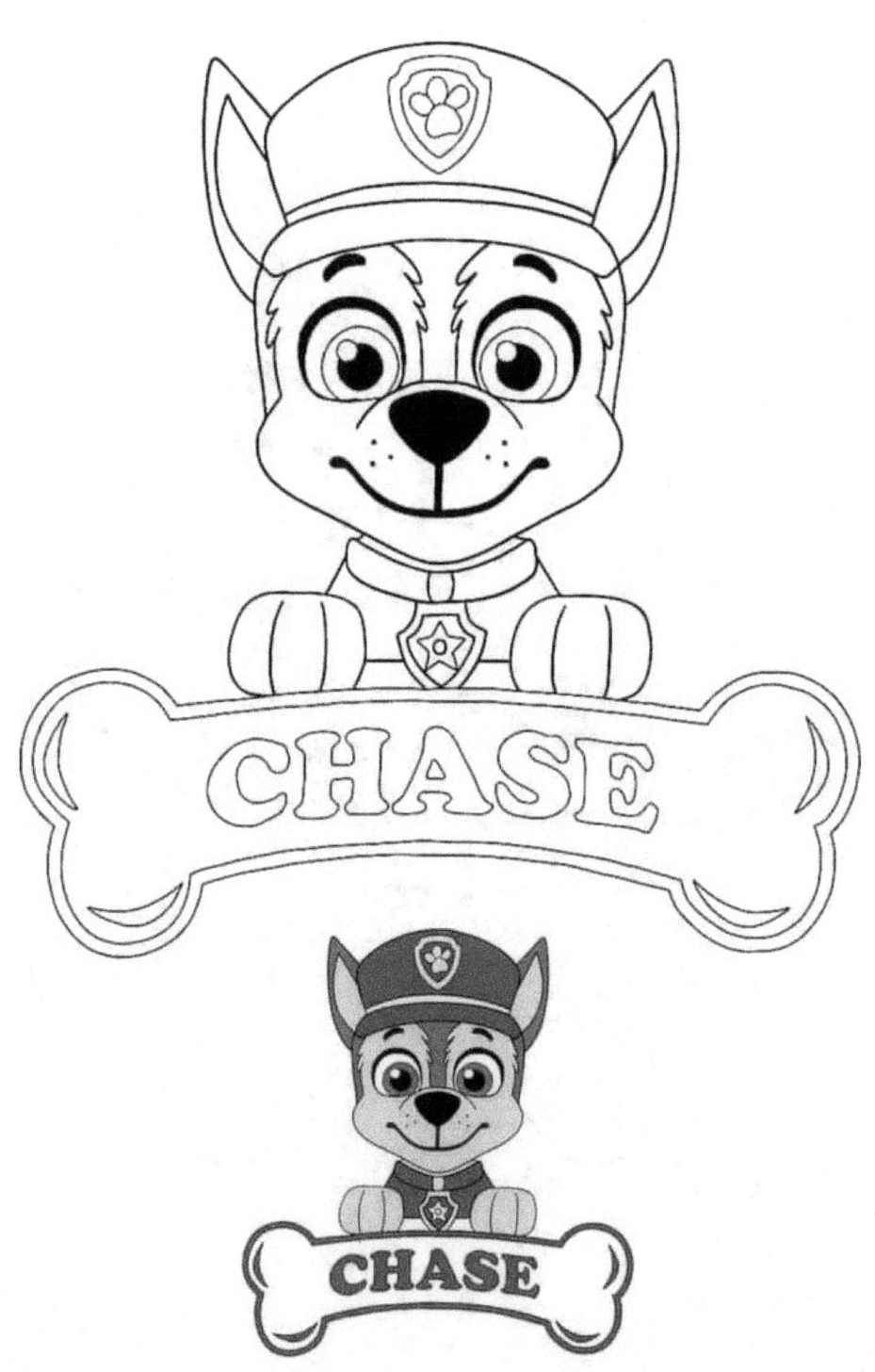

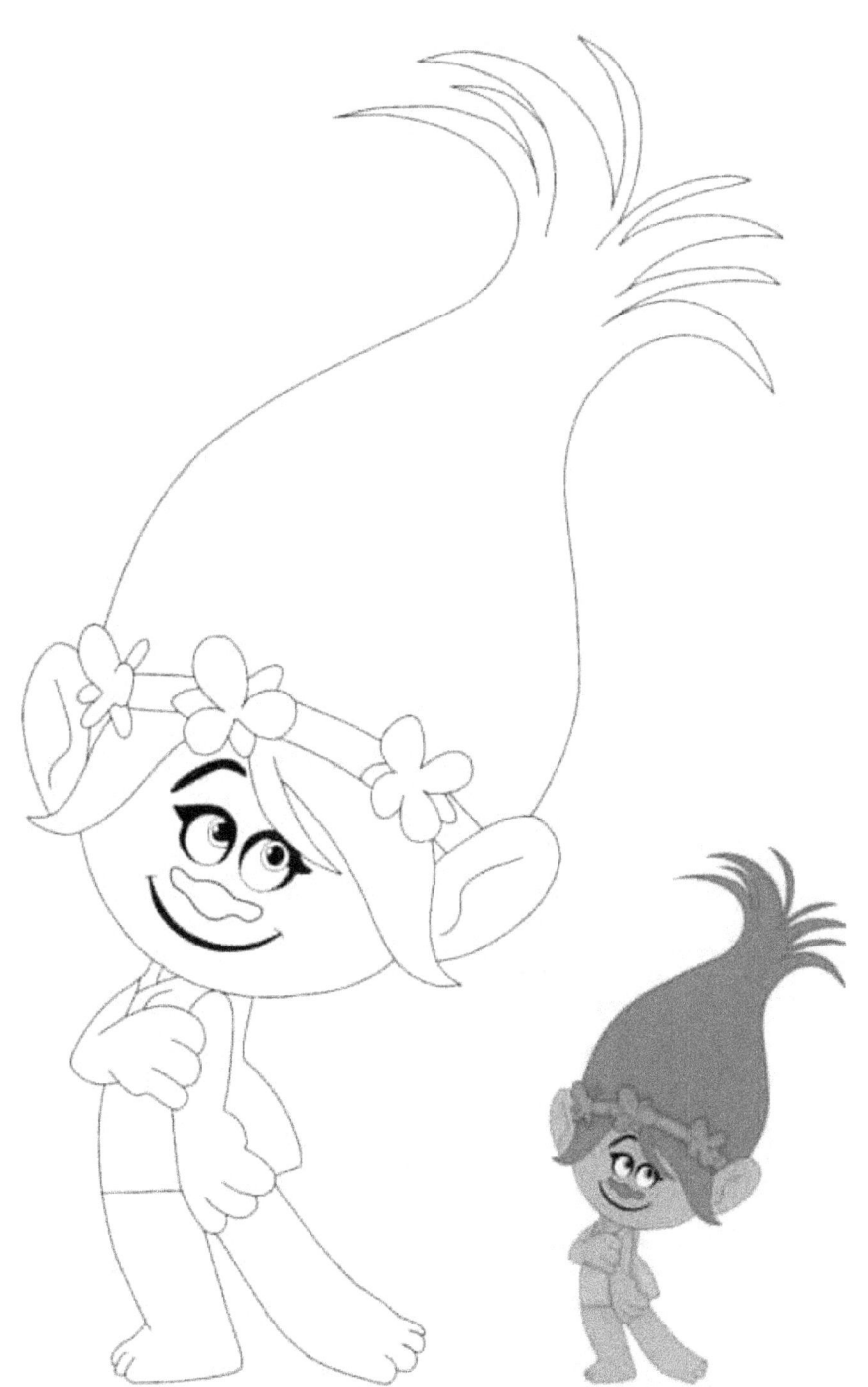

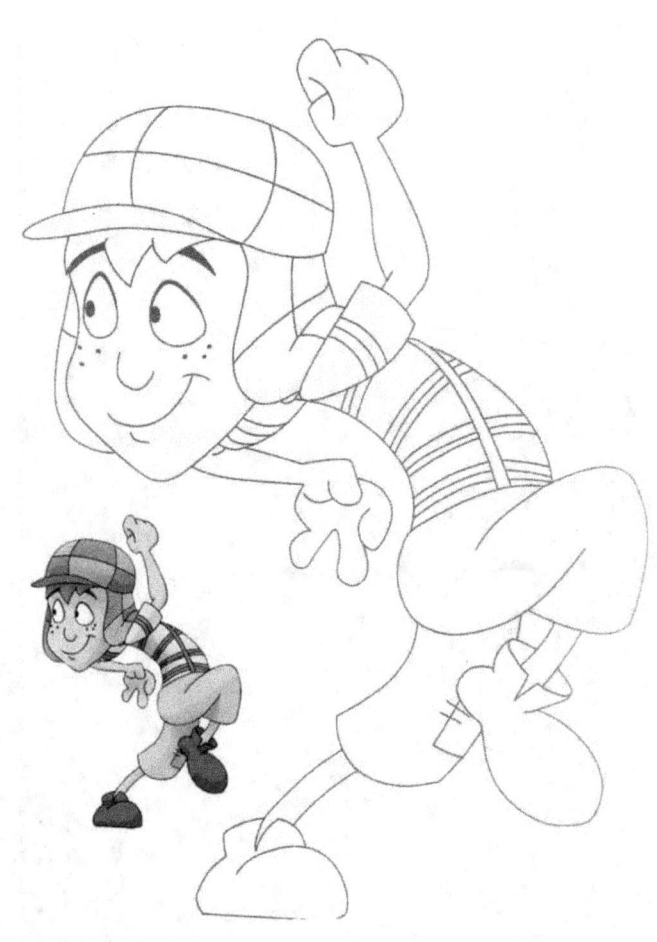

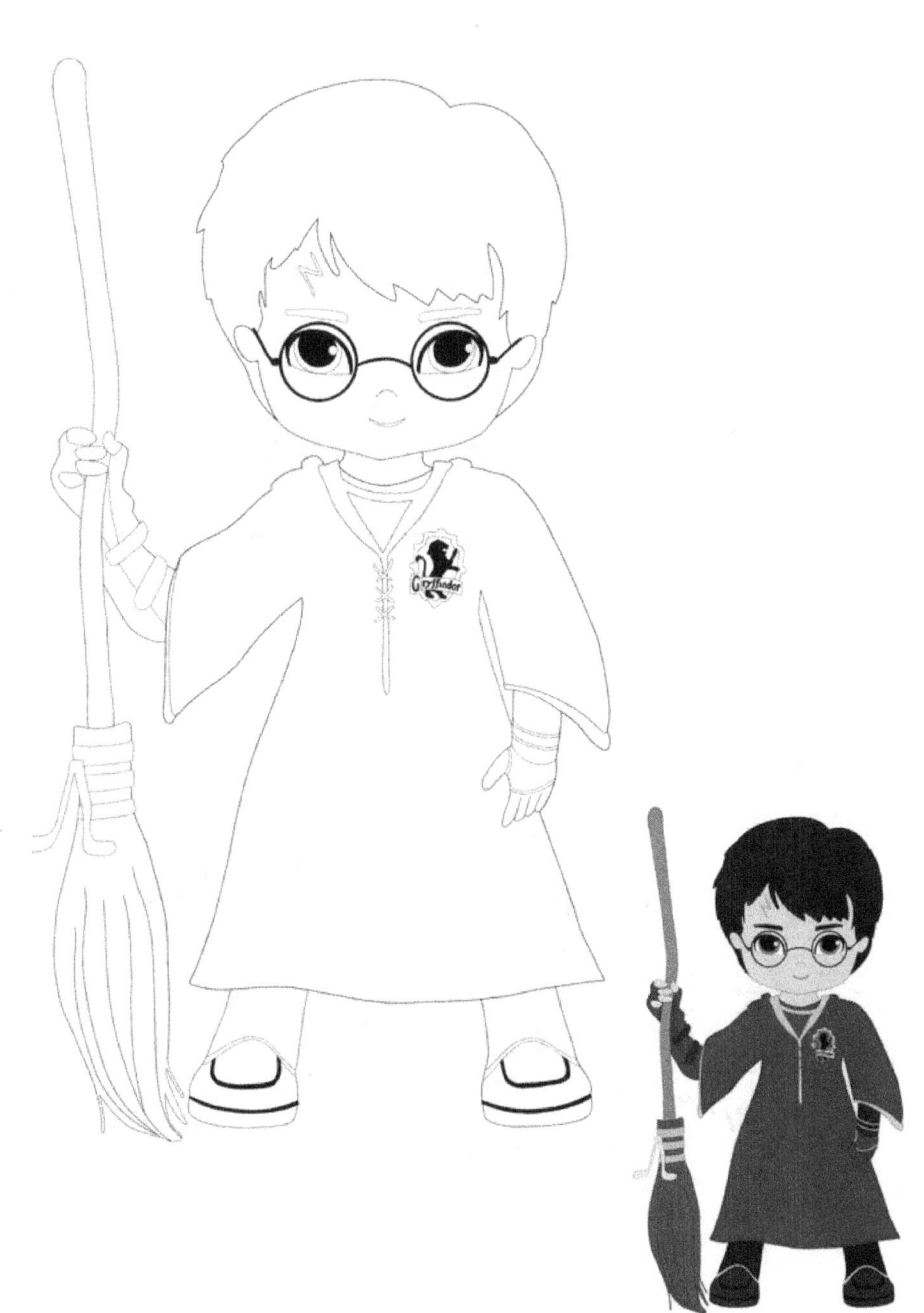

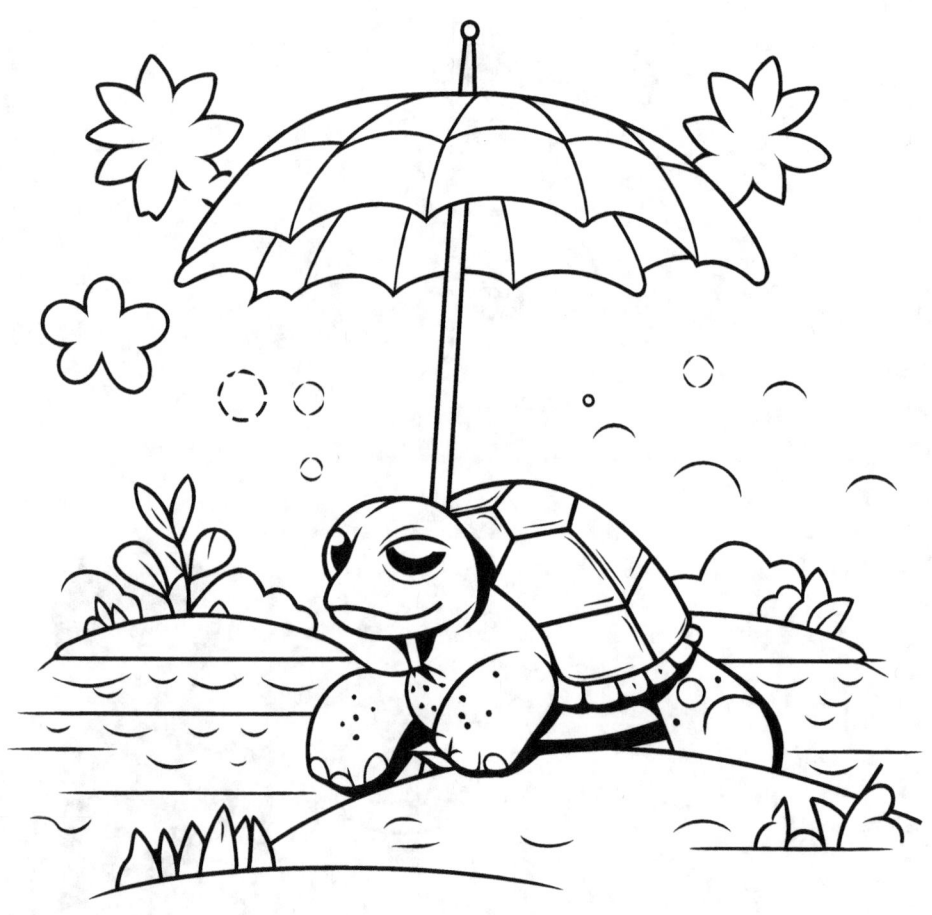

www.ingramcontent.com/pod-product-compliance
Lightning Source LLC
Chambersburg PA
CBHW062237220526
45471CB00009B/3514